LIONEL MESSI

BY LEIGH LEWIS

AMICUS LEARNING

Inspire is published by
Amicus Learning, an imprint of Amicus
P.O. Box 227
Mankato, MN 56002
www.amicuspublishing.us

Editor: Ana Brauer
Series Designer: Kathleen Petelinsek
Book Designer and Photo Researcher: Emily Dietz

Library of Congress Cataloging-in-Publication Data
Names: Lewis, Leigh, author.
Title: Lionel Messi / By Leigh Lewis.
Description: Mankato, MN : Amicus Learning, [2026] | Series: Inspire | Includes bibliographical references and index. | Audience: Ages 5–9 | Audience: Grades 2–3 | Summary: "Learn about soccer star Lionel Messi and his accomplishments in an engaging profile packed with photos and fact-filled text suitable for young readers. Includes table of contents, glossary, further resources, and index" — Provided by publisher.
Identifiers: LCCN 2024044109 (print) | LCCN 2024044110 (ebook) | ISBN 9798892005210 (library binding) | ISBN 9798892005753 (paperback) | ISBN 9798892006293 (ebook)
Subjects: LCSH: Messi, Lionel, 1987—Juvenile literature. | Soccer players—Argentina—Biography—Juvenile literature.
Classification: LCC GV942.7.M398 L48 2026 (print) | LCC GV942.7.M398 (ebook) | DDC 796.334092—dc23/eng/20241209
LC record available at https://lccn.loc.gov/2024044109
LC ebook record available at https://lccn.loc.gov/2024044110

Photo Credits: Alamy Stock Photo/Aflo Editorial, 12, ColomboPics, 6, ZUMA, 7; Associated Press/Francisco Seco, 4, Ricardo Mazalan, cover, Tom Weller/picture-alliance/dpa, 13; Getty Images/El Grafico, 9, Hector Vivas, 19, JUAN MABROMATA, 16–17, Julian Avram/Icon Sportswire, 14, Michael Regan - EMPICS, 10, TIMOTHY A. CLARY, 8, Vaughn Ridley, 20; Shutterstock/Remo_Designer, 11

Table of Contents

Lionel Messi is one of the greatest soccer players of all time.

A Soccer Superstar

Lionel Messi gets the ball. He runs past one defender. Then another. Then another. He shoots. The goalie dives but misses. The ball finds the corner of the net. GOAL!

Lionel Messi is a soccer superstar from Argentina.

NICKNAMES

Messi's nicknames are Leo and La Pulga Atomica (the Atomic Flea).

Grandma's Support

In 1991, Messi started playing at a club called Grandoli. He was four. The coach was worried. He thought Messi would get hurt. Messi's grandma convinced the coach to let her grandson play. She was always Messi's biggest fan.

Messi (front row, second from right) started playing for Newell's Old Boys when he was eight.

NOB

DID YOU KNOW?
In 1995, Messi switched clubs to join Newell's Old Boys. He played with his brother.

Time to Grow

In 1999, Messi was diagnosed with a **growth hormone deficiency** (GHD). He was only 4 feet 4 inches (1.32 meters) tall. A year later, he was signed by a club in Spain. He was 13. FC Barcelona paid for his GHD treatments.

En Barcelona a 14 de Diciembre del 2000
y en presencia de los Sres. Minguella y Horacio
Carlos Rexach Secretario Técnico del F.C.B.
se compromete bajo su responsabilidad y
a pesar de algunas opiniones en contra
a fichar al jugador Lionel Messi siempre.
y cuando nos mantengamos en las
cantidades acordadas

Fdo.

DID YOU KNOW?
The agreement for Messi to move to Spain was written on a paper napkin.

Messi's GHD was cured. He grew to be 5 feet 7 inches (1.7 m) tall.

Messi played with Barcelona for 17 years.

Going Pro

In 2004, Messi played in his first professional game. Barcelona beat RCD Espanyol 1–0. Messi was 17. He played for only seven minutes. His teammates said they knew he'd be the best in the world.

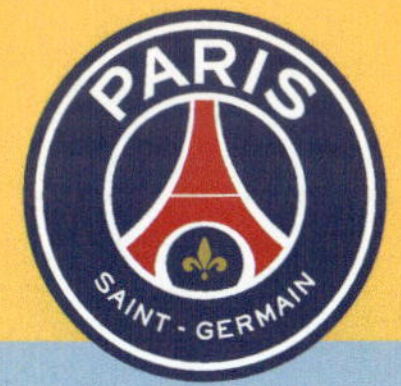

TEAM PLAYER

In 2021–22, Messi switched teams to play for Paris Saint-Germain FC. In 2023, he started playing for Inter Miami CF in the US.

World Cup Champion

In the World Cup, players play for their home countries. In 2022, Argentina beat France in the final. They won during **penalty shootouts**. Messi won the Golden Ball award. It was for the best player in the World Cup.

WINNING THE GOLD
Messi helped lead Argentina to win a gold medal at the 2008 Beijing Olympics.

Messi cheers with his team after winning the 2022 World Cup.

In 2023, Messi signed a two and a half year contract with Inter Miami CF in Florida.

The Messi Show

Messi is like a magician on the field. He makes plays happen out of nothing. He **dribbles** the ball with the outside of his foot. He uses body **feints** to trick defenders. He scores goal after goal.

DID YOU KNOW?
Messi is left-handed and shoots with his left foot.

Messi and his wife have three sons (left to right), Mateo, Ciro, and Thiago.

Family Man

Messi is married and has three sons. He first met his wife, Antonela Roccuzzo, when he was five years old. They reconnected in 2005 and married in 2017. He tries to enjoy every second with his family.

Making the World a Better Place

Messi started the Leo Messi **Foundation**. It focuses on healthcare and children in need. He donates money. He goes to important events. He believes there are more important things in life than winning a game.

Messi signs autographs before a match.

Messi plays the ball during a game in 2024.

The G.O.A.T.

Messi has won more trophies than any other soccer player. He won best player for Argentina. He won best player for his club teams. He truly is the greatest soccer player of all time.

SUPER STATS

LIONEL ANDRÉS MESSI CUCCITTINI

Birthday: June 24, 1987

Hometown: Rosario, Argentina

Position: Forward

Professional club teams played for: Spain's FC Barcelona, France's Paris Saint-Germain FC, USA's Inter Miami CF

ACCOMPLISHMENTS

Olympic Gold Medalist: 2008

World Cup winner: 2022

Record holder of Ballon d'Or Awards: 2009–2012, 2015, 2019, 2021, 2023

Record holder of The Best FIFA Football Awards: 2009–2012, 2015, 2019, 2022, 2023

Record appearances as World Cup captain: 19

GLOSSARY

dribble To move the ball forward on the ground while keeping control of it.

feint A false movement that is meant to trick an opponent by taking attention away from the real target.

foundation An organization set up to help others by giving money or services.

growth hormone deficiency A treatable condition that causes short height.

penalty shootouts When a game ends in a tie, teams take turns shooting a goal from the penalty mark, with only the goalie defending the goal.

READ MORE

Buckley Jr., James. **Who is Lionel Messi?** Penguin Workshop, 2024

Sánchez Vegara, Maria Isabel. **Leo Messi.** Frances Lincoln Children's Books, 2023.

ON THE WEB

Britannica Kids: Lionel Messi
https://kids.britannica.com/students/article/Lionel-Messi/627581

Lionel Messi Homepage
https://messi.com/en/

INDEX

About the Author

Leigh Lewis is a children's author who loves her three kids, traveling, pickleball, and telling stories. She has lived in the US, Russia, Japan, England, Greece, and Turkey. Check out her books at leighlewisbooks.com.